CRYPTS, TOMBS, AND SECRET ROOMS

THE PYRAMIDS OF GIZA

BY ENZO GEORGE

Gareth Stevens
PUBLISHING

Please visit our website, www.garethstevens.com. For a free color catalog of all our high-quality books, call toll-free 1-800-542-2595 or fax 1-877-542-2596.

Cataloging-in-Publication Data
Names: George, Enzo.
Title: The pyramids of Giza / Enzo George.
Description: New York : Gareth Stevens Publishing, 2018. | Series: Crypts, tombs, and secret rooms |
    Includes index.
Identifiers: ISBN 9781538206607 (pbk.) | ISBN 9781538206546 (library bound) | ISBN 9781538206423 (6 pack)
Subjects: LCSH: Pyramids of Giza (Egypt)--Juvenile literature. | Jizah (Egypt)--Antiquities--Juvenile literature.
Classification: LCC DT63.G47 2018 | DDC 932--dc23

Published in 2018 by
Gareth Stevens Publishing
111 East 14th Street, Suite 349
New York, NY 10003

For Brown Bear Books Ltd:
Managing Editor: Tim Cooke
Designer: Lynne Lennon
Editorial Director: Lindsey Lowe
Children's Publisher: Anne O'Daly
Design Manager: Keith Davis
Picture Manager: Sophie Mortimer

Picture credits:
Cover: WitR
Interior: 123rf: Sergei Butorin 39, Thomas Wyness 38, Elena Yurkina 37; **Bibliothequé Nationale de France:** Nadar 32; **Dreamstime:** 15, 42, Mahmoud Mahdy 40, Alex Zarubin 41; **Library of Congress:** 26, 34, 35, 36; **Metropolitan Museum of Art:** 28; **Public Domain:** 25, 27, 33, Corbis 24, Millennial Dawn 30, Hans Hillwaert 31; **Shutterstock:** 10, Gurgen Bakhshetyan 6b, Stphen Chung 18, Andrea Izzotti 43, Brian Maudsley 7; **Thinkstock:** Johan Andersson 11, Chameleonseye 19, Dorling Kindersley 14, 16, Victoria G. 13, istockphoto 9, 20, 23, 29, Photos.com 8, 22, Zoonar 5.

All other images Brown Bear Books

Brown Bear Books has made every attempt to contact the copyright holder.
If anyone has any information please contact licensing@brownbearbooks.co.uk

Printed in the United States of America
CPSIA compliance information: Batch CS17GS: For further information contact Gareth Stevens, New York, New York at 1-800-542-2595.

CONTENTS

WORDS IN THE GLOSSARY APPEAR IN BOLD TYPE THE FIRST TIME THEY ARE USED IN THE TEXT.

GUARDIANS OF THE DESERT

On the outskirts of Cairo, Egypt's capital city, three **pyramids** rise out of the desert at a place called Giza. The pyramids are the oldest of the Seven Wonders of the Ancient World and the only one that still survives. The Great Pyramid of Khufu is the largest of the pyramids. For more than 4,000 years after it was completed in about 2560 BC, the Great Pyramid was the tallest structure on Earth.

Of the nearly 100 pyramids that stand along the Nile River in Egypt, only the Great Pyramid is known to have chambers and passageways inside. No full body or mummy has ever been found inside a pyramid. Yet the pyramids are some of the most spectacular tombs ever constructed. They are memorials to the rulers, or pharaohs, of early Eygpt — and to the ancient Egyptians' interest in death and the **afterlife**.

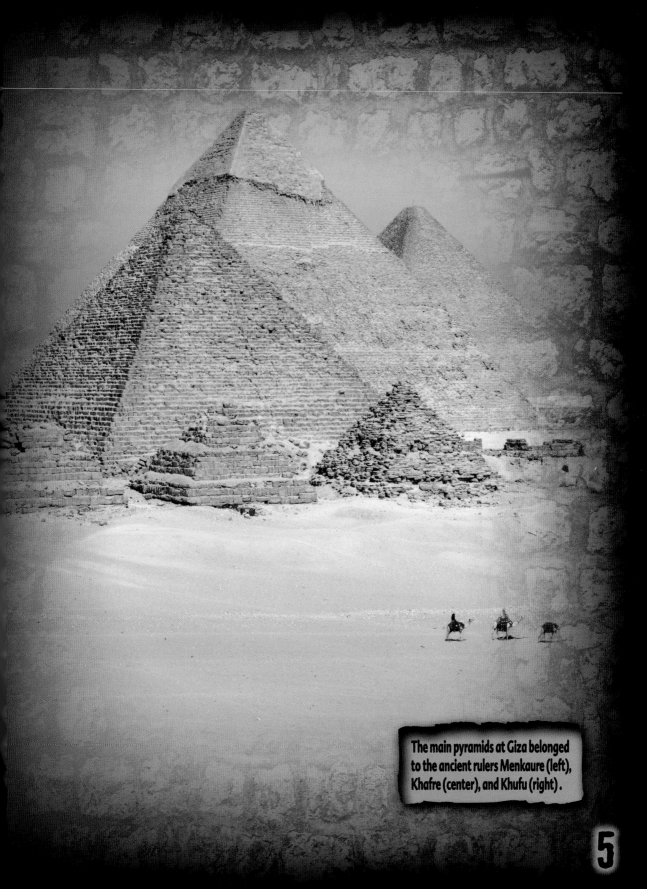

The main pyramids at Giza belonged to the ancient rulers Menkaure (left), Khafre (center), and Khufu (right).

STONES OF THE PAST

The pyramids at Giza are very old. Experts think the oldest, the Great Pyramid, is at least 4,500 years old. It belonged to King Khufu (also known as Cheops), who ruled Egypt around the 2500s BC. Khufu built his pyramid on the Giza plateau, across the Nile from his capital at Memphis. The second pyramid at Giza belonged to his son, Khafre. The last to be built, and the smallest, belonged to Khafre's son, Menkaure. Giza is also home to three smaller pyramids that likely belonged to queens, and to the huge statue called the Sphinx. There are also temples, smaller tombs, and pits where boats were buried.

The Great Sphinx is believed to have the face of Pharaoh Khafre. It guards his pyramid at Giza (center).

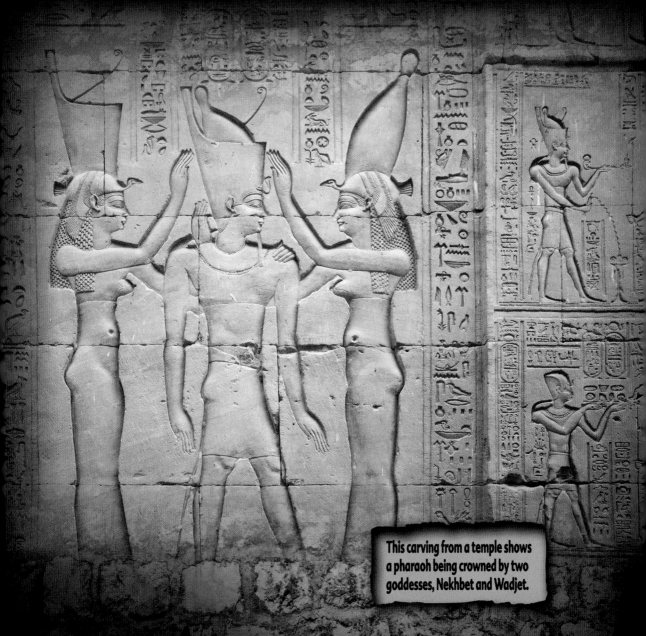

This carving from a temple shows a pharaoh being crowned by two goddesses, Nekhbet and Wadjet.

A DIVINE RULER

The Egyptians believed their ruler was **divine**. They saw him or her as a representative of the sun god, Ra. When a pharaoh died, he or she returned to Ra in the sky. A tall pyramid was thought to help the pharaoh make that journey. The dead pharaoh would also need his possessions in the afterlife, so they were buried with him.

The walls of wealthy tombs were painted with scenes and spells to help the dead person find the way to the underworld.

ANCIENT EGYPTIAN BURIALS

ANCIENT EGYPTIANS BELIEVED IN AN AFTERLIFE, SO THEY BURIED THE DEAD WITH ALL THE POSSESSIONS THEY WOULD NEED AFTER DEATH, INCLUDING FOOD TO EAT AND INSTRUCTIONS TO HELP THEM REACH THE UNDERWORLD. THE POOR WERE BURIED WITH FEW IF ANY OBJECTS, BUT MORE IMPORTANT PEOPLE WERE BURIED WITH GREAT TREASURES. THE EGYPTIANS BELIEVED THE DEAD WOULD NEED THEIR BODIES IN THE AFTERLIFE. THEY PRESERVED BODIES IN A PROCESS CALLED MUMMIFICATION AND PERFORMED RELIGIOUS CEREMONIES TO ENSURE THAT THE DEAD PERSON WOULD BE PERMITTED TO ENTER THE AFTERLIFE.

TOWARD THE FIRST PYRAMID

The Egyptians believed the dead needed their bodies after death. From about 2600 BC, they began to **mummify** the bodies of high-ranking officials. These officials were buried with their possessions in small brick buildings known as **mastabas**. However, mastabas were easy targets for grave robbers, who often struck as soon as a burial was over.

In the 2600s BC, Pharaoh Djoser asked his **architect**, Imhotep, to create a new type of tomb. Imhotep built a **step pyramid**, and Djoser was buried with his possessions in underground chambers beneath the structure. The chambers failed to stop robbers, however. The tomb was soon emptied. Today all that remains of Djoser, who was king during the 3rd **dynasty**, is his mummified left foot.

The step pyramid built by Imhotep for the Pharaoh Djoser still stands in the desert at Saqqara.

PYRAMIDS TAKE OFF

In the mid-2500s BC, a pharaoh named Snefru, the father of Khufu, built a step pyramid. It originally had seven levels, but Snefru increased that to eight levels. Snefru then abandoned the step pyramid for a second pyramid with smooth sides, but after 30 years' work the new pyramid started to sink into the soft ground.

It was only after Snefru had built his third smooth-sided pyramid (the Red Pyramid) that builders learned enough skills to successfully complete the second pyramid. They positioned the stone blocks more precisely, and built the top of the four sloping walls at a shallower angle. The finished pyramid has an obvious "bend" that gives it its nickname of the Bent Pyramid—but today it is in better shape than many pyramids built at the same time.

The point where Snefru's builders changed the angle of the Bent Pyramid is clearly visible.

The Great Sphinx was carved out of a ridge of limestone on the plateau at Giza.

THE GREAT SPHINX

FACING THE RISING SUN AT GIZA IS A HUGE STONE STATUE WITH A LION'S BODY AND THE FACE OF A PHARAOH, BELIEVED TO BE KHAFRE. EGYPT HAS MANY SIMILAR STATUES, OR SPHINXES, OF LIONS' BODIES WITH THE HEADS OF HUMANS. KHAFRE'S SPHINX, HOWEVER, IS FAR LARGER THAN ANY OTHER, AT ABOUT 66 FEET (20 M) HIGH! IT WAS PROBABLY BUILT TO GUARD KHAFRE'S PYRAMID. IN THE NEW KINGDOM (16TH–11TH CENTURIES BC), THE SPHINX WAS PROBABLY WORSHIPPED AS A FORM OF THE SUN GOD, RA.

BUILDING THE MONUMENTS

More than 1,000 years after the pyramids were built at Giza, ancient Egyptians themselves could not figure out how the monuments had been built. Despite centuries of archaeological investigation, experts still do not know exactly how the pyramids were constructed.

Many experts believe blocks were raised to the top of pyramids by being dragged along huge ramps.

The pyramids stood close to the Nile, so that stone and supplies could be transported to the site by water.

A HUGE WORKFORCE

It is clear that it must have taken a huge construction force to build a pyramid. Experts believe that it took at least 5,000 men more than 20 years to build the Great Pyramid of Khufu. There was an easy supply of labor, however. As the **absolute ruler**, the pharaoh could command his subjects to work on the site. He may have used farmers when they were not busy with the harvest, or soldiers from the army during peacetime.

Building a pyramid required different skills. Many men helped to provide the materials for construction. Millions of stones were dug from nearby **quarries**, while special stone such as granite or the polished limestone that covered the outside of the pyramid came from farther away. The stone was transported to Giza by barge along the Nile. All the stones had to be cut into blocks and polished before being raised into position. Each block was sealed into place using a mixture of sand and cement called mortar.

Other laborers built ramps and **embankments** to allow stones to be carried up the monument. Metalworkers cut tools, while carpenters made sledges to transport goods and potters made pots for cooking food and carrying water. Bakers, brewers, and cooks supplied the builders.

THE ANNUAL FLOOD

The number of workers on the site was at its highest during the annual flood of the Nile. In late summer and early fall each year, the Nile overflowed its banks. Unable to work in their flooded fields, farmers came to work on the pyramids until the waters receded. Experts believe that at these times the number of workers on site swelled to as many as 25,000. Workers probably considered it an honor to work on a pyramid, because they saw the pharaoh as a god.

The masons who shaped the stone left their own unique marks to identify which blocks they worked on.

The sun sets behind the Giza pyramids on the outskirts of the modern city of Cairo, Egypt's capital.

SELECTING A SITE

PYRAMIDS WERE BUILT ON THE WEST SIDE OF THE RIVER NILE. THE SUN SET IN THE WEST, SO IT IS LIKELY THIS WAS WHERE THE EGYPTIANS BELIEVED THE DEAD ENTERED THE UNDERWORLD. THE SITE AT GIZA WAS PROBABLY CHOSEN BECAUSE IT WAS A LARGE, ROCKY PLATEAU THAT COULD SUPPORT THE IMMENSE WEIGHT OF THE STRUCTURES. IT WAS HIGH ENOUGH ABOVE THE RIVER TO ESCAPE THE ANNUAL FLOODS, BUT CLOSE ENOUGH FOR THE NILE TO BE USED TO TRANSPORT BLOCKS OF BEST-QUALITY LIMESTONE AND GRANITE FROM TURA ON THE OPPOSITE BANK. GIZA HAD ITS OWN SUPPLY OF ROCK CLOSE BY FOR THE MAIN PART OF THE STRUCTURE. IT WAS ALSO CLOSE TO THE ANCIENT EGYPTIAN CAPITAL OF MEMPHIS, SO THE PHARAOH COULD INSPECT HIS PYRAMID WHENEVER HE WANTED.

Sleds, rollers, and ropes were used to drag the stones over the sand and up ramps to the top of the pyramid.

In addition to the laborers, there were also many overseers, engineers, and architects. The most important person on the site was the king's personal architect. It was his job to translate the pharaoh's wishes into reality.

CLEARING THE SITE

Before building began, the architect and his engineers drew accurate plans. Workers then prepared the **foundations** by removing any sand to reveal the **bedrock** beneath. Before any stones could be laid, the base had to be flat. That was a huge task. To build the Great Pyramid, for example, required flattening an area of 2,800 square yards (2,341 sq m). Workers may have dug channels and used them to flood the area to show where any rock was sticking up above the water level. Once the water drained away, the rock was cut back in some places or built up in others until it was completely flat.

A MOUNTAIN OF STONE

Once the base was flat, the workers could begin building the pyramid. The Great Pyramid contains around 7 million tons (6.35 million tonnes) of stone, with each block weighing between 2 and 17 tons (2–15 tonnes). In order to complete construction during Khufu's reign, a block would have had to have been produced every 2 minutes every day for 23 years.

The main stone for construction was quarried close to Giza. At the time, ancient Egyptians did not use the wheel. In order to move the heavy stones, workers tied them to sleds.

Workers haul stones up a pyramid as they prepare to fill in its original steps to create smooth sides.

The pyramids are believed to have been built as tall as possible in order to help the dead pharaoh reach the sky, which was thought to be the home of Ra, the sun god.

Workers dragged the sleds on wooden rollers. In order to reduce **friction**, a worker likely poured water onto the sand to keep it damp enough for the rollers to glide over it. As the pyramid grew, the stones had to be lifted into place. The builders did not have any kind of crane. Instead, experts think they built different types of mud-brick ramps to roll the stones higher up the pyramid.

STAGES OF CONSTRUCTION

The workers first built the central core of the pyramid. Around this core, they built stepped walls to **buttress** the immense weight. The steps were filled with packing blocks to create smooth sides. The outer walls were finished with a layer of casing stones that fit precisely together. The casing stones were carved from highly polished limestone. They would have given the pyramid a shiny appearance, almost like a giant mirror. At the top, the four walls were crowned by a four-sided, pointed **capstone**. Although the Great Pyramid is missing its capstone, Khafre's pyramid still has its pointed top.

THE CAPSTONE

THE MOST IMPORTANT PART OF THE PYRAMID WAS THE CAPSTONE AT ITS PEAK. THE CAPSTONE BROUGHT THE FOUR SIDES OF THE PYRAMID TO A POINT AND GAVE THE WHOLE STRUCTURE ITS DISTINCTIVE SHAPE. BECAUSE IT WAS SO IMPORTANT, THE CAPSTONE WAS MADE OF POLISHED PRECIOUS STONE OR EVEN GOLD. TODAY, ALTHOUGH KHAFRE'S PYRAMID STILL HAS ITS CAPSTONE, THE CAPSTONE OF THE GREAT PYRAMID IS MISSING. WAS IT LOOTED SOMETIME IN THE DISTANT PAST, OR WAS IT BUILT WITHOUT ONE? WE HAVE NO WAY OF KNOWING.

The capstone of the Great Pyramid has been missing since ancient times.

SECRETS OF THE PAST

Since they were built more than 4,000 years ago, the pyramids of Giza have refused to give up their secrets. Their builders did not leave any records to explain why they built them. Experts have theories, or ideas, but do not know for sure. Since ancient times, people have wondered what the pyramids were for. In particular, people wonder about the Great Pyramid of Khufu.

The Great Pyramid (right) looks smaller than its companions in this image, but this is an optical illusion.

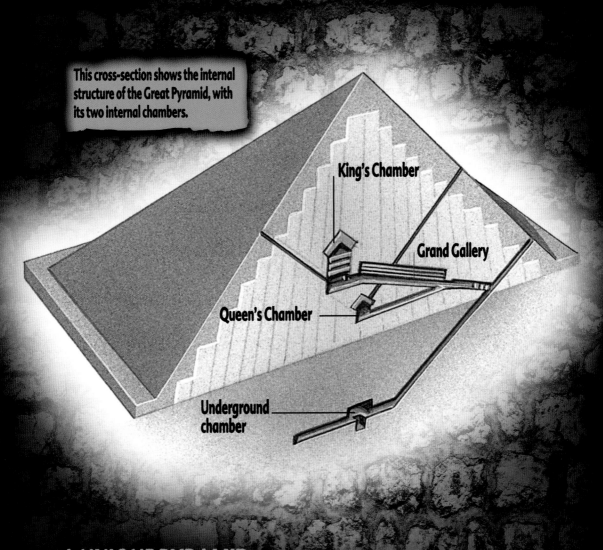

This cross-section shows the internal structure of the Great Pyramid, with its two internal chambers.

King's Chamber

Grand Gallery

Queen's Chamber

Underground chamber

A UNIQUE PYRAMID

Around 100 pyramids still stand in Egypt. What makes the Giza pyramids special is both their age and their remarkable size. Their construction was the outstanding technical feat of ancient Egypt. The skill of the pyramid builders reached its peak in the Great Pyramid. It is the only pyramid known to have a complex internal structure. No previous pyramid had been as ambitious as Khufu's — and all later pyramids were poor copies of his achievement.

UNLIKELY SUGGESTIONS

ARCHAEOLOGISTS BELIEVE THE PYRAMIDS WERE BUILT AS TOMBS FOR THE PHARAOHS, BUT OTHER PEOPLE HAVE SUGGESTED DIFFERENT PURPOSES FOR THE STRUCTURES. THEORIES INCLUDE THAT THE PYRAMIDS WERE AN ASTRONOMICAL OBSERVATORY, A PLACE FOR ELABORATE RITUALS, GRAIN STORES, AND A DEVICE TO COMMUNICATE WITH EXTRATERRESTRIALS. SOME PEOPLE HAVE EVEN ARGUED THAT THE PYRAMIDS WERE NOT BUILT BY THE ANCIENT EGYPTIANS AT ALL, BUT BY PEOPLE FROM ATLANTIS, A MYTHICAL CITY SAID TO HAVE VANISHED BENEATH THE OCEAN.

This illustration shows Egyptian astronomers observing the night sky from a passage in a pyramid.

WHAT'S INSIDE?

The builders of the Great Pyramid originally created an entrance on the north side about 56 feet (17 m) above the ground. The entrance was later covered with casing stones. It led to a narrow, low tunnel known as the Descending Passage, which slopes at an angle of 26 degrees. The passage is 344 feet (105 m) long, but only 3.5 feet (1 m) wide and 4 feet (1.2 m) high. It leads to a chamber dug out of the rock beneath the pyramid. What was the purpose of this chamber? Some experts have suggested that it was intended to hold the pharaoh's **sarcophagus**. The passage is so narrow and low, however, that it would be hard to move a sarcophagus along it.

The Grand Gallery leads up through the heart of the pyramid toward the so-called King's Chamber.

Partway along the Descending Passage from the entrance is a plug of granite in the ceiling. It blocks the entrance to a second tunnel, known as the Ascending Passage because it slopes upward. This Ascending Passage slopes at a 26-degree angle, like the Descending Passage, and is the same size. An adult would be too tall to stand up in the passage, so the only way to move along it is by bending over. What might the passage have been used for?

THE GRAND GALLERY

After crawling along the Ascending Passage for about 124 feet (38 m), a visitor arrives suddenly in a large, tall space where it is easy to stand upright. This is the Grand Gallery. Its walls are made of polished limestone and it is about 26 feet (8 m) tall and 7 feet (2 m) wide.

At the start of the Grand Gallery, a horizontal passage leads deep inside the pyramid to a chamber known as the Queen's Chamber — although it was not meant for a queen! Arab explorers who opened the pyramid in the 800s called it the Queen's Chamber because it had a **gabled** roof, like the tombs in which Arab women were buried.

The Queen's Chamber appears unfinished. The first explorers to find it noted that the walls were covered in salt. But where the salt came from is a mystery, and today the salt has been cleared.

The chamber is empty now but medieval explorers said it held a granite box. They said the box was not decorated, which was unusual. The Egyptians carved **hieroglyphs** on many monuments and objects. A pharaoh's sarcophagus was highly decorated, so the box in the Queen's Chamber was probably not Khufu's coffin.

This granite plug (top) seals the entrance from the Descending Passageway to the Ascending Passageway.

25

EARLY AIR-CONDITIONING

WAS THE KING'S CHAMBER COOLED BY AN EARLY FORM OF AIR-CONDITIONING? TWO NARROW SHAFTS, OR TUNNELS, EXTEND FROM THE NORTH AND SOUTH WALLS OF THE CHAMBER OVER 200 FEET (60 M) TO THE OUTSIDE OF THE PYRAMID. THE PURPOSE OF THE SHAFTS IS A MYSTERY. SOME EXPERTS BELIEVE THEY MIGHT HAVE BEEN INTENDED TO ALLOW FRESH AIR INTO THE CHAMBER. WHEN THE TWO SHAFTS WERE CLEANED AND OPENED DURING THE 1800s, IT WAS DISCOVERED THAT THEY HELPED KEEP THE CHAMBER AT A CONSTANT TEMPERATURE OF 68°F (20°C).

An Egyptian guide stands in the entrance to the Great Pyramid in this photograph taken by an American tourist in the 1920s.

THE BIGGEST MYSTERY

At the top of the Grand Gallery is the "Great Step," a huge stone from where a passage leads to a small **antechamber**. There, a huge suspended slab partly blocks the entrance to a flat-ceilinged chamber at the heart of the pyramid. Because the Arabs buried men in flat-roofed tombs, the first explorers named this the King's Chamber.

The chamber is made from 100 granite blocks. The only object inside is a chocolate-colored granite box without a lid. The box is too big to have been placed inside the chamber after the pyramid was built.

If this was the resting place of Khufu, where are the other possessions buried with him? And where is the pharaoh's body? Like nearly everything about the interior of Khufu's Great Pyramid, the answer is still a mystery.

INVESTIGATING THE PAST

For thousands of years, travelers, explorers, and archaeologists have puzzled over the purpose of the pyramids. The last pyramids were built sometime around 1700 BC. By the time the Egyptian civilization was conquered by the Romans about 1,600 years later, even the Egyptians themselves had forgotten why their distant ancestors had built the huge monuments.

EARLY VISITORS

The pyramids fascinated the ancient Greeks. As early as the 500s BC, Thales of Miletus visited Giza. Thales was a Greek philosopher, or thinker, who discovered many parts of geometry, the branch of math concerned with the study of shapes. Thales wanted to figure out how tall the Great Pyramid was.

The ancient Greek historian Herodotus reported that the pyramids were built by slaves, but modern experts believe he was mistaken.

The Egyptian queen Cleopatra (left) married the Roman Mark Antony, leading to Egypt's invasion by the Romans in 30 BC.

Thales did this by measuring its shadow. He stuck a stick into the ground and waited until its shadow was the same length as the stick. At that moment, the length of the pyramid's shadow would be the same as the pyramid's height. Thales could measure the pyramid's shadow, adding on half the width of the pyramid's base. He estimated the structure was 481 feet (147 m) tall. Today it is 455 feet (139 m) tall. It has shrunk due to **erosion**.

The next important ancient Greek to visit Giza was the historian Herodotus in the mid-400s BC. His writings helped to shape the ideas people still have about the pyramids.

Herodotus got his information by talking to priests in the temples associated with the pyramids. But the priests were describing things that had happened nearly 2,000 years earlier. Their accounts may well have been unreliable.

The Romans conquered Egypt in 30 BC and ruled it until their empire fell in AD 476. Soon after the fall of Rome, Egypt became a Muslim country. The only Europeans who visited Giza were Christian **pilgrims**. They called the pyramids Joseph's grain stores, refering to the Bible story of Joseph saving Egypt from starvation.

ARAB RULE

The Arabs conquered Egypt in AD 642. Around 180 years later Caliph Abdullah Al Mamun ordered his men to investigate the Great Pyramid. They failed to find an entrance, so they dug straight into the side of the pyramid for over 100 feet (30 m).

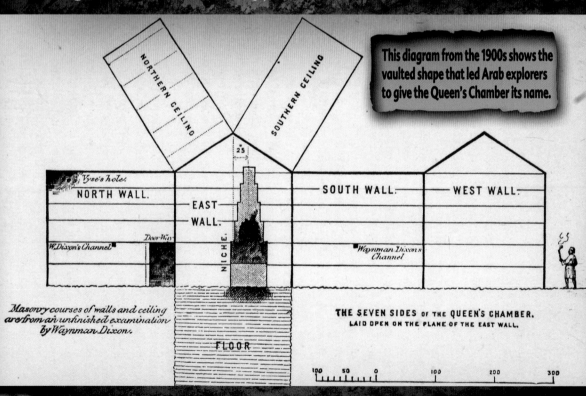

This diagram from the 1900s shows the vaulted shape that led Arab explorers to give the Queen's Chamber its name.

NORTHERN CEILING

SOUTHERN CEILING

25

Vyse's hole.
NORTH WALL.

EAST WALL.

SOUTH WALL.

WEST WALL.

Door Way

W. Dixon's Channel

NICHE.

Waynman Dixon's Channel

Masonry courses of walls and ceiling are from an unfinished examination by Waynman Dixon.

FLOOR

THE SEVEN SIDES OF THE QUEEN'S CHAMBER.
LAID OPEN ON THE PLANE OF THE EAST WALL.

100   50   0   100   200   300

They were about to give up when they found the Descending Passage, which they described as incredibly dark and difficult to get through. They discovered and named the King's and Queen's chambers. The Great Pyramid even appeared in the famous collection of folk stories called *The Arabian Nights*. In the story, the pyramid had magical powers and held great treasures.

Over the years, many stones have been stripped off the pyramids. It is thought that builders used the ready-shaped stones to build the city of Cairo.

REDISCOVERY

It was only in the 1700s that Europeans again began to take an interest in Egypt, which was then a remote part of the Ottoman Empire. **Missionaries** trying to convert people to Christianity started visiting Egypt, but it was the arrival of the French general Napoleon Bonaparte in 1798 that started a European craze for everything connected with ancient Egypt.

Napoleon Bonaparte's men found the Rosetta Stone in 1799. It helped people decipher Egyptian hieroglyphs.

Bonaparte was one of the rulers of France after its revolution. His expedition to Egypt was planned to damage British trade there and the trade routes to Britain's colony in India. Bonaparte took scientists and artists to Egypt to help **catalog** its ancient treasures. Among the finds was the Rosetta Stone. This stone was key to improving our understanding of ancient Egypt.

The Rosetta Stone was carved with the same text in three forms of writing, including hieroglyphs. Nearly 20 years later, a French scholar named Jean-François Champollion used the other writing on the stone to translate the hieroglyphs. For the first time, the picture writing could now be understood by scholars.

HELP YOURSELF!

After Napoleon's visit, Europeans flocked to Egypt. They took any traces of the ancient civilization they could find. **Artifacts**, statues, and even mummies were taken back to Europe. In the 1800s it was not illegal to remove **antiquities** from another country.

Auguste Mariette was one of the first archaeologists to carry out well-planned excavations, or digs, at Giza.

BONAPARTE IN EGYPT

AFTER AN EARLY DEFEAT BY ENGLISH FORCES IN EGYPT, NAPOLEON'S EXPEDITION ENDED UP STAYING THERE FOR THREE YEARS. THE EXPERTS NAPOLEON HAD GATHERED TO MAKE A DETAILED RECORD OF EGYPT HAD PLENTY OF TIME TO WORK. FRENCH SURVEYORS MEASURED AND STUDIED THE GIZA PYRAMIDS AND DETAILED DRAWINGS APPEARED IN THE 20-VOLUME *DESCRIPTION OF EGYPT* PUBLISHED AFTER THE EXPEDITION. OVERNIGHT, EVERYONE WANTED TO SEE THE PYRAMIDS FOR THEMSELVES.

This painting of Napoleon and his chief of staff in Egypt was created by Jean-Léon Gérôme in 1863.

Guides help a tourist to climb up the outside of the Great Pyramid in the early 1900s.

In 1853, the French **Egyptologist** Auguste Mariette found the Valley Temple, part of the funerary complex that included Khafre's pyramid. The temple was buried beneath the sand. Mariette spent the next five years clearing its interior. The temple was in good condition, but experts still do not know precisely what it was for. Some people believe that this was where Khafre's body was turned into a mummy. Other experts think that important ceremonies were carried out there after the pharaoh died in order to prepare his soul for the afterlife.

THE FATHER OF EGYPTOLOGY

IN THE LATE 1800s THE ENGLISHMAN WILLIAM MATTHEW FLINDERS PETRIE PIONEERED A NEW WAY OF STUDYING THE PYRAMIDS AND OTHER EGYPTIAN RUINS. PETRIE THOUGHT THAT SITES SHOULD BE PRESERVED AS THEY WERE FOUND SO THAT EXPERTS MIGHT UNDERSTAND THEM BETTER. HE SPENT YEARS SURVEYING AT GIZA AND FIGURING OUT HOW THE PYRAMIDS WERE BUILT. IN 1883, HE PUBLISHED HIS RESEARCH IN AN INFLUENTIAL BOOK, *THE PYRAMIDS AND TEMPLES OF GIZEH*.

Crumbling blocks made climbing the pyramids very difficult. Today, climbing on the stones is forbidden.

THE MONUMENTS TODAY

The pyramids of Giza still dominate the skyline of the modern city of Cairo. Recent archaeological discoveries have added to the world's knowledge of the structures — but the pyramids have still not given up all their secrets.

US sailors visit the Great Sphinx in the late 1890s, before the statue was cleared of the sand that had buried it.

Giza is one of the most visited ancient sites not only in Egypt but throughout the world.

A POPULAR DESTINATION

One of the most famous visitors to enter the King's Chamber was Napoleon after he invaded Egypt in 1798. One story says that Napoleon asked to be left alone there. When he left, he seemed upset. He ordered his men not to mention the visit again. When Napoleon was on his deathbed, a friend asked him what had happened inside the pyramid. Napoleon refused to say. He said that his friend would never believe him.

Along with the burial site of the later Egyptian pharaohs including Tutankhamun at the Valley of the Kings near Luxor in southern Egypt, the pyramids of Giza are Egypt's most popular tourist destination. Today, tourists can go inside the Great Pyramid and visit the King's Chamber

INVESTIGATING THE MONUMENTS

Before the 1900s, few visitors to Giza understood the importance of preserving the site. They destroyed many objects in their hunt for valuables. Over the years, stones have been stripped from the pyramids. In the 1830s, a British archaeologist even tried to blast an entrance into the Great Pyramid using gunpowder!

Today, protection of the pyramids is a priority. The many visitors to the site bring valuable money to Egypt, but they also cause damage. Their feet wear away the rock, so people have been forbidden from climbing on the pyramids. The breath of thousands of visitors has increased **humidity** levels inside the Great Pyramid. The damper air this creates threatens to damage the ancient walls.

Crowds of Egyptian and foreign visitors present problems for experts trying to preserve the ancient site.

Tourists crowd into an Egyptian burial chamber. Moisture in people's breath threatens to damage ancient walls.

STRANGE FORCES

SOME PEOPLE WHO VISIT THE KING'S CHAMBER TODAY CLAIM TO EXPERIENCE ODD PHENOMENA, SUCH AS STRANGE LIGHTS OR VISIONS. SUCH STORIES HAVE ONLY ADDED TO THE MYSTERY SURROUNDING THE GREAT PYRAMID AND THE GIZA COMPLEX. MOST EXPERTS DISMISS ANY SUPERNATURAL EXPLANATIONS OF SUCH STORIES. IT MAY BE SIMPLY THAT VISITORS ARE EXHAUSTED BY THE TIME THEY REACH THE KING'S CHAMBER, AND THEIR MIND PLAYS TRICKS ON THEM. THE CLIMB THROUGH THE ASCENDING PASSAGE IS STEEP, NARROW, AND LOW. EVEN THOUGH THE GRAND GALLERY IS FAR TALLER, THE CLIMB TO THE KING'S CHAMBER IS STILL VERY STEEP — AND IT IS NOT FOR ANYONE WHO SUFFERS FROM CLAUSTROPHOBIA.

New sites were discovered at Giza throughout the 1900s. In 1925, the only grave goods known at Giza were found in the tomb of Khufu's mother, Queen Hetepheres, east of the Great Pyramid. The tomb contained wooden furniture covered in gold material.

In 1954, a full-size boat that it is thought was intended to take Khufu to the afterlife was found in a pit south of his pyramid. It had been taken apart and buried. Over the next 13 years, experts reconstructed the vessel, which is now housed in a museum next to the pyramid at Giza.

MORE DISCOVERIES

In recent decades, archaeologists found a bakery where artisans made bread for the workers. They have even found 600 skeletons of the workers themselves. Their graves were found in 1990 when a tourist's horse tripped over a stone in the desert. The skeletons showed that some men had been injured in accidents on the site. Some had signs of surgery to treat their injuries.

It is thought that Khufu's sun boat was intended to help him sail to the afterlife in the same way that the sun sailed across the sky.

Khufu's boat is so large that it has been left in position next to the Great Pyramid in its own specially built museum.

From analyzing the skeletons, experts figured out that the men were between 30 and 35 years old when they died. The men were buried with bread and jars of beer for the afterlife. Experts say this suggests that they were free citizens rather than slaves.

NEW TECHNOLOGY

Archaeologists use the latest methods to investigate the pyramids. In 1993 and 2002, they sent crawling robots with caterpillar tracks and cameras inside the Great Pyramid.

A ROBOT DOES THE JOB

IN 1993, A ROBOT NAMED UPUAUT WAS USED TO EXPLORE THE AIRSHAFTS IN THE QUEEN'S CHAMBER. SINCE THE 1800S, PEOPLE HAD KNOWN THAT THE NARROW SHAFTS FROM THE KING'S CHAMBER LED TO THE OUTSIDE OF THE PYRAMID. THEY HAD LOCATED THE EXIT HOLES ON THE SIDES OF THE STRUCTURE. BUT NO EXIT POINTS HAD BEEN FOUND FOR THE SHAFTS FROM THE QUEEN'S CHAMBER. WOULD THE ROBOT BE ABLE TO DO THE JOB? UPUAUT CRAWLED ALONG ONE SHAFT FOR ABOUT 200 FEET (61 M) BEFORE IT WAS STOPPED BY A STONE DOOR. IN 2002, ANOTHER ROBOT DRILLED THROUGH THE DOOR AND FOUND ANOTHER DOOR WITH METAL PINS. NO ONE KNOWS WHAT LIES BEYOND THE SECOND DOOR, BUT IT SEEMS UNLIKELY THE SHAFT REACHES THE OUTSIDE OF THE PYRAMID. IN WHICH CASE, WHAT WAS IT FOR?

One of the greatest remaining mysteries about the pyramids is what happened to the mummies of the kings for whom they were built as tombs.

The robots were used to explore the narrow shafts that lead out from the two chambers. These shafts run north–south rather than on the east–west alignment of the rising and setting sun. Experts guessed they were for ventilation.

Inside the shafts, the robots filmed hieroglyphs in red paint and carvings made by the builders of the pyramid. One shaft was blocked by a door-like panel. In 2002, the Pyramid Rover robot drilled a tiny hole in the panel and pushed its camera through. It found a small chamber with another panel with metal attachments that resembled door handles, but which did not seem to have any practical purpose.

A NEW MYSTERY

Experts now think that the shafts may have been designed for a **symbolic** purpose and not as airshafts. However, no one knows what the purpose might have been. Even though we know more about the pyramids than ever before, much about them remains a mystery.

Egypt's rulers were buried in a carved sarcophagus, but none has ever been found in the pyramids at Giza.

TIMELINE

BC

2600s The pharaoh Djoser of Egypt's 3rd Dynasty orders his architect, Imhotep, to construct a step pyramid in the desert at Saqqara. The ancient Egyptians also begin to mummify their dead in order to preserve them.

2500s The pharaoh Snefru of the 4th Dynasty has three pyramids built. The third, called the Red Pyramid, is usually seen as the first true, or smooth-sided, pyramid. Later, Pharaoh Khufu (also known as Cheops) builds the Great Pyramid at Giza

c.2490 Khufu's son, Khafre, builds his own pyramid next to that of his father. The statue of the Great Sphinx, which is believed to represent Khafre, was probably also built around this time.

c.2470 Khafre's son, Menkaure, builds the smallest of the three pyramids at Giza.

c.1700 The last pyramids are built in Egypt. Later pharaohs are usually buried in hidden tombs in the Valley of the Kings.

500s The Greek Thales of Miletus visits the pyramids. He measures the height of the Great Pyramid by using its shadow.

400s The Greek historian Herodotus visits the pyramids and writes down what priests tell him about their creation.

30 Egypt becomes part of the Roman Empire.

AD

642   Arabs take control of Egypt.

c.820   Workers of Caliph Al Mamun explore the Great Pyramid and find the internal chambers and passageways.

1798   The French general Napoleon Bonaparte leads an expedition to Egypt that surveys and records many of its ancient structures.

1799   French soldiers discover the Rosetta Stone. It will later help experts to decipher the hieroglyphs.

1830s   A British adventurer uses gunpowder to try to blast a hole in the Great Pyramid.

1853   French archaeologist Auguste Mariette discovers a new temple at Giza.

1883   William Matthew Flinders Petrie publishes *The Pyramids and Temples of Gizeh*.

1954   Khufu's sun boat is discovered and reassembled at Giza.

1990   The graves of more than 600 workers who built the pyramids are discovered by chance.

1993   The robot Upuaut explores the Great Pyramid.

2002   The Pyramid Rover continues the exploration of the Great Pyramid.

Note on dates: Experts disagree about dates from ancient Egypt, including when pharaohs reigned. The dates shown here are commonly accepted, but other sources may give different dates.

GLOSSARY

absolute ruler A monarch who has no limits on his or her power.

afterlife Life after death.

antechamber A small room leading to a main one.

antiquities Objects or buildings from the ancient past.

archaeologists People who study history by examining old structures and artifacts.

architect Someone who designs and constructs buildings.

artifacts Objects that have been made by people.

bedrock Solid rock beneath loose soil or sand.

buttress To strengthen a wall with additional support.

capstone A pointed, four-sided stone on top of a pyramid.

catalog To make a systematic record of something.

divine Associated with a god.

dynasty A series of rulers from the same family. Egypt's history is measured in dynasties.

Egyptologist Someone who studies ancient Egypt.

embankments Walls or banks made of earth.

erosion The process of being worn away by wind or water.

foundations The lowest parts of a building that hold up the rest of it.

friction Resistance caused when two surfaces rub together.

gabled Having a triangular-shaped ceiling or roof.

hieroglyphs Writing symbols that use little pictures to represent objects or sounds.

humidity The amount of moisture in the air.

mastabas Room-like stone tombs.

missionaries People who try to make converts to a religion.

mummify To preserve a body by drying it out.

pilgrims People who travel to a sacred site as a religious act.

pyramids Structures with a square base and four sides that rise to a point.

quarries Places where stone is dug from the ground.

sarcophagus A stone coffin, which is usually decorated.

step pyramid A pyramid built in a series of separate layers.

symbolic Describes something that represents something else.

FURTHER INFORMATION

Books

Deady, Kathleen W.
Ancient Egypt: Beyond the Pyramids (Great Civilizations). Mankato, Minn: Capstone Press, 2012.

Hoobler, Thomas and Dorothy.
Where Are the Great Pyramids? (Where Is?). New York: Grosset and Dunlap, 2015.

Morley, Jacqueline.
You Wouldn't Want to Be a Pyramid Builder (You Wouldn't Want to... Ancient Civilizations). New York: Franklin Watts, 2014.

Stanborough, Rebecca.
The Great Pyramid of Giza (Engineering Wonders). Mankato, Minn: Capstone Press, 2016.

Websites

www.ducksters.com/history/ancient_egypt/great_pyramid_of_giza.php
A Ducksters.com page about the Great Pyramid at Giza.

http://www.softschools.com/facts/wonders_of_the_world/great_pyramid_of_giza_facts/66/
This page from Soft Schools has a list of fascinating facts about the Great Pyramid.

http://kids.nationalgeographic.com/explore/history/seven-wonders/#Pyramids-at-Giza.png
This page from National Geographic for Kids has facts about the Seven Wonders of the Ancient World.

INDEX